WHAT TO DO WHEN YOU GET DUMPED

Also by Suzy Hopkins and Hallie Bateman

What to Do When I'm Gone

Also by Hallie Bateman

Brave New Work
Directions
Eggasaurus (illustrator)

WHAT TO DO WHEN YOU GET DUMPED

A guide to

UNBREAKING

your heart

SUZY HOPKINS & HALLIE BATEMAN

BLOOMSBURY PUBLISHING
NEW YORK · LONDON · OXFORD · NEW DELHI · SYDNEY

BLOOMSBURY PUBLISHING
Bloomsbury Publishing Inc.

1385 Broadway
New York
NY 10018
USA

BLOOMSBURY, BLOOMSBURY PUBLISHING, and the Diana logo
are trademarks of Bloomsbury Publishing Plc

First published in the United States 2025

ISBN: HB: 978-1-63973-189-3
eBook: 978-1-63973-190-9

Library of Congress Cataloging-in-Publication Data is available

2 4 6 8 10 9 7 5 3 1

Designed and typeset by Myunghee Kwon
Printed in China by C&C Offset Printing Co., Ltd., Shenzhen, Guangdong

To find out more about our authors and books visit
www.bloomsbury.com and sign up for our newsletters.

Bloomsbury books may be purchased for business or promotional use.
For information on bulk purchases please contact Macmillan Corporate
and Premium Sales Department at specialmarkets@macmillan.com.

If you need a thread of hope to mend a tattered heart,
this book is for you.

WHAT TO DO
WHEN YOU GET
DUMPED

Introduction

Welcome to your new life: the one you didn't ask for, didn't want, and never expected.

This book is for those who, having loved and trusted another human being, have been unceremoniously and unequivocally dumped. Tossed like last week's leftovers, a bag of trash, a nonswimmer thrown free of the boat without warning into a cold, hard sea.

It hurts when you hit that cold water. And the safety of the shore is nowhere in sight: You may be splashing and flailing, near drowning, in fact, for some time. Weeks, months, years.

When it happened to me—my husband of thirty years announcing starry-eyed that he'd reconnected with a former girlfriend (a marriage counselor, no less)—I fell into a deep pit of disbelief, horror, grief, anger, and abject misery.

At times I thought that my heart might stop from the pain of it all. Followed by this thought: Maybe that wouldn't be such a bad thing.

I wanted to understand other people's experiences. How did they shed this despair and move on? I read books (the most useful were on grief linked to death), but none felt deeply relevant to my situation. And I perused online forums, to no avail other than a grim sense of solidarity. Most stories were so much sadder than mine, particularly when young children were involved, that I sometimes just wrote a note of encouragement.

But I needed my own note, one that would help me believe I could make it through to a new life, with as many specifics as possible. I wanted to know steps A, B, and C, and if possible, D through Z.

I didn't want to lose myself in drugs or alcohol, or in some new relationship before I knew what happened to this one. I wanted instead to find myself again, the person I left behind decades ago, misplaced after a long and toxic dance with an out-of-sync and uninterested partner.

This book emerged as a way to process my own grief, a pep talk of sorts written three years in as I began to know what to make of it all. I hope that it offers you a note of encouragement, the one I wish I'd had.

Suzy Hopkins

DUMPEE BILL OF RIGHTS

You the Dumped, in order to unbreak your heart, hold these inalienable rights:

- You have the right to express yourself fully and honestly.

- You have the right to say "no" to whomever or whatever does not help you move forward.

- You have the right to grieve and heal in a way that works for you and you alone, for as long as it takes.

KEY

X = The Dumper (your ex)

Y = X's new love interest, if there is one

Countdown = Time it takes to get over X (my count is in days; I hope yours will be in hours)

PART I

The End

If you're exceptionally hardy, force a smile and tell yourself this is a new adventure. More likely, yesterday's pain will suffuse you like a toxic cloud: What just happened?

Countdown: 1,582 days

PANIC

I could tell you not to, but let's face it: You're probably going to panic. Every cell in your body may want to scream. True, there are stoic types for whom this dumping may constitute a little setback, worthy of a quiet tear or two amid moments of somber reflection.

But if you're like me, you will sweat profusely, double over, shriek, cry, vomit, all while thinking that this is the end of the world. It is not—but it feels like it. During this panic phase, stop screaming periodically to practice patches of slow breathing, and slow counting.

When you fall to the floor, stay in the fetal position for as long as needed. Then roll over onto your back and slowly count ceiling tiles or cobwebs or actual spiders. Do it out loud, to hear the sound of a human voice that's not leaving you. Let the floor gently hold you until your legs are up to the task.

KEEP PANICKING

Where will I live? How will I survive financially? What will this do to my children? Will anyone ever love me again? Am I going crazy? Who can I talk to? What now? What next? When will I wake up from this nightmare? Why is this happening to me? How did I not see this coming?

Any one of these can be terrifying. Each will be answered in time. Right now, just know that so many other people have felt this same fear yet made it through. You will too.

MAKE A TO-DO LIST

You're in shock, so keep your goals simple. Make a small list, something to check off so that you'll feel better about accomplishing nothing. If it's a workday, put your clothes on and show up (it's enough).

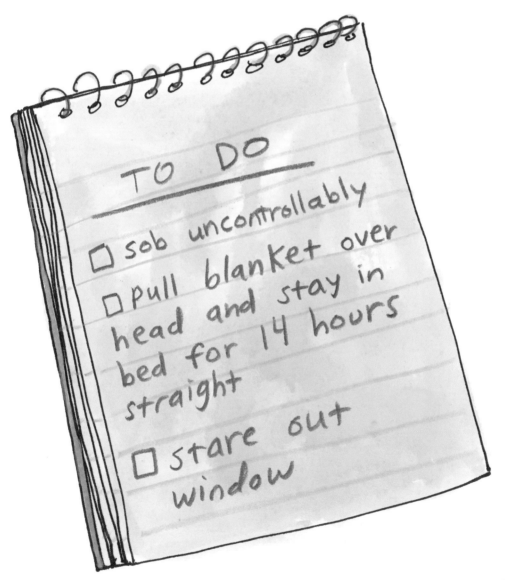

CUE THE MONTAGE

Sometimes during traumatic events, time seems to slow as your brain records the unfolding action frame by painful frame. Those images may flip through your head for days on end, looping relentlessly in the locked-door theater of your mind. What X said, what X did, the indifference, the unreality, the finality, the disbelief: This can't be real.

Meanwhile, thoughts of X will swirl endlessly:
What is X doing? Does X miss me? Is X banging Y right now?

Eventually this film loop will stop. One day in the distant future—please trust me on this—you will be getting ready for bed and realize, "I only thought about X twice today!" And later, perhaps not at all. At some point, your thoughts will shift to your own life, and the people you love who love you back.

Be patient.

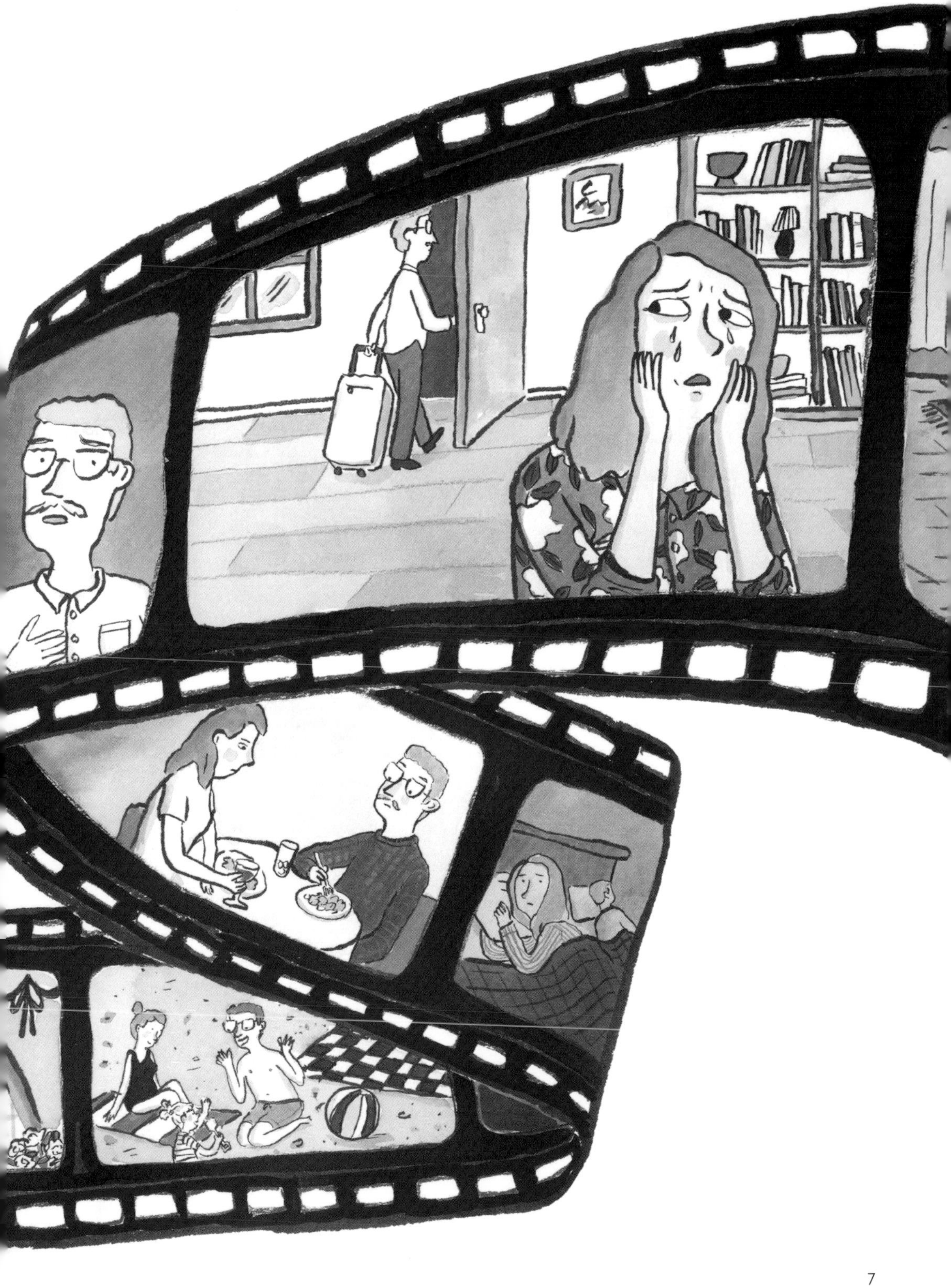

CLIMB ABOARD

You've been given a one-way ticket on the pain train, destination unknown, and there are so many decisions ahead. But not today. Today the only thing you have to do is make it through the next few hours.

Keep in mind that although you feel like its only passenger, the pain train is actually packed. People the world over get dumped, multitudes every day. Nice people, nasty people. Beautiful people, ugly people, people of all faiths and predilections.

TAKE COVER

If you've been together for a short time, emotions and living arrangements may be entwined but little else. After years of partnership, things get more complicated: kids, finances, possessions, pets, family relationships, and social networks.

You lose not just the person but the life you shared and the future you imagined: the children you might have or planned to have, the home you created, retirement journeys, grandchildren you'd dote on together.

Sudden severance of a relationship can feel like the terrifying last-minute unraveling of a parachute you thought would keep you safe; you survive the crash, but barely. Later you'll slowly start work on a new chute (and a backup) made of stronger material. But that's in the future. Now it's time to take cover in the safest place you can find.

If other people can help with that, by making you feel a bit less alone, call them. If you need to crawl into a dark closet with a pile of blankets, do that instead.

Note: Don't forget to feed your children,
dog, cat, or parakeet.
They're not responsible
for this mess.

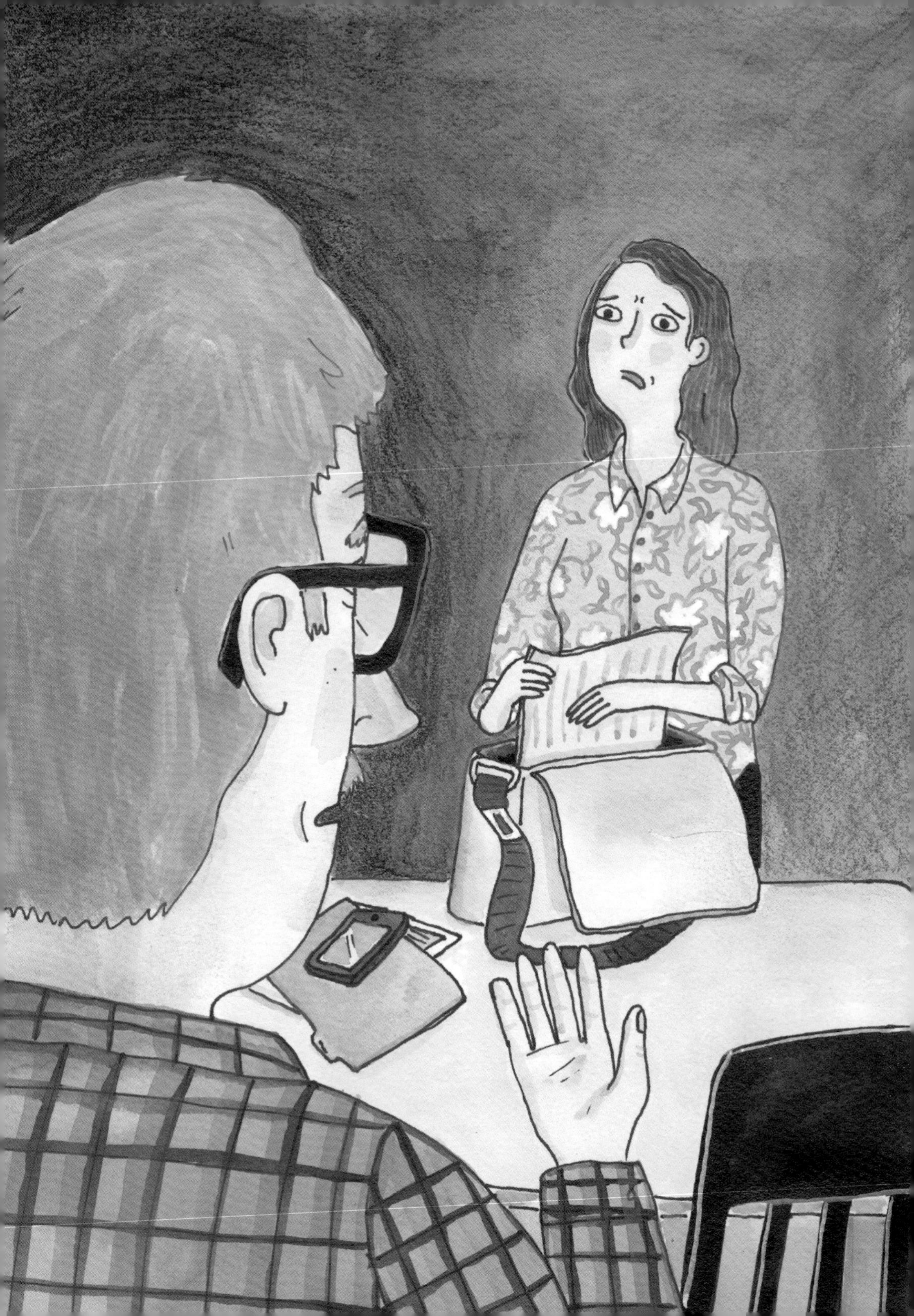

Countdown: 1,577 days

FLASHBACK

The memory of that day continues to cycle.

I'm getting ready to go to the office, already late, wrapping up my years in the working world two days before X and I go on a long-planned trip to celebrate my retirement.

X has something to tell me. "You're so smart," he says, "you'd find out anyway." Not that smart, apparently. This is all news to me.

With a glazed look, not unhappy—more dreamy-eyed—X reveals a series of phone calls rekindling a relationship with Y from thirty years earlier. This movie of the way he initially told me flickered for weeks in my brain, always with the soundtrack of my frantic heartbeat, fear, and anger—my sympathetic nervous system (what a good name) offering fight or flight. I chose flight that morning, driving to work in shock, helping to deny reality until I could handle it.

Once activated, that fight-or-flight response may continue at high rev for a long time. With no one else there, you eventually discover that you can't run from yourself. You are the one who needs your attention now.

Countdown: 1,576 days

FORGET LOGIC

Whatever led X to leave you may exist far beyond the realm of logic. As inclined as you are to try to make sense of it all—rationale, sequence of events, words said or not said—data analysis will not help. Gone is gone.

WALK IN CIRCLES

There's a reason people pace the floor during difficult times. It puts a cadence to the discord. When you are sinking into the depths, take a walk until mood-boosting endorphins kick in, however long that takes.

Walking in circles—say, around a school running track, or out in the woods where no one can hear you scream—can imprint the understanding that endings are beginnings and beginnings are endings. And yes, I know you're way too sad right now to appreciate that philosophical byway. It will make more sense later on.

PREPARE FOR AFTERSHOCKS

If X gives you a letter a few days later about the agony they're experiencing, set it aside unopened for a year. But since I know you'll ignore that advice, here's what to expect: You'll read it with scalded eyes, throw it on the floor, and for weeks afterward be unable to cleanse your mind of gems like "I hope we can be friends."

A few days later, back to pick up some belongings, X may restate how difficult this split is for them, the terrible angst they're experiencing, admitting in a voice heavy with heartache: "God, I miss the dogs."

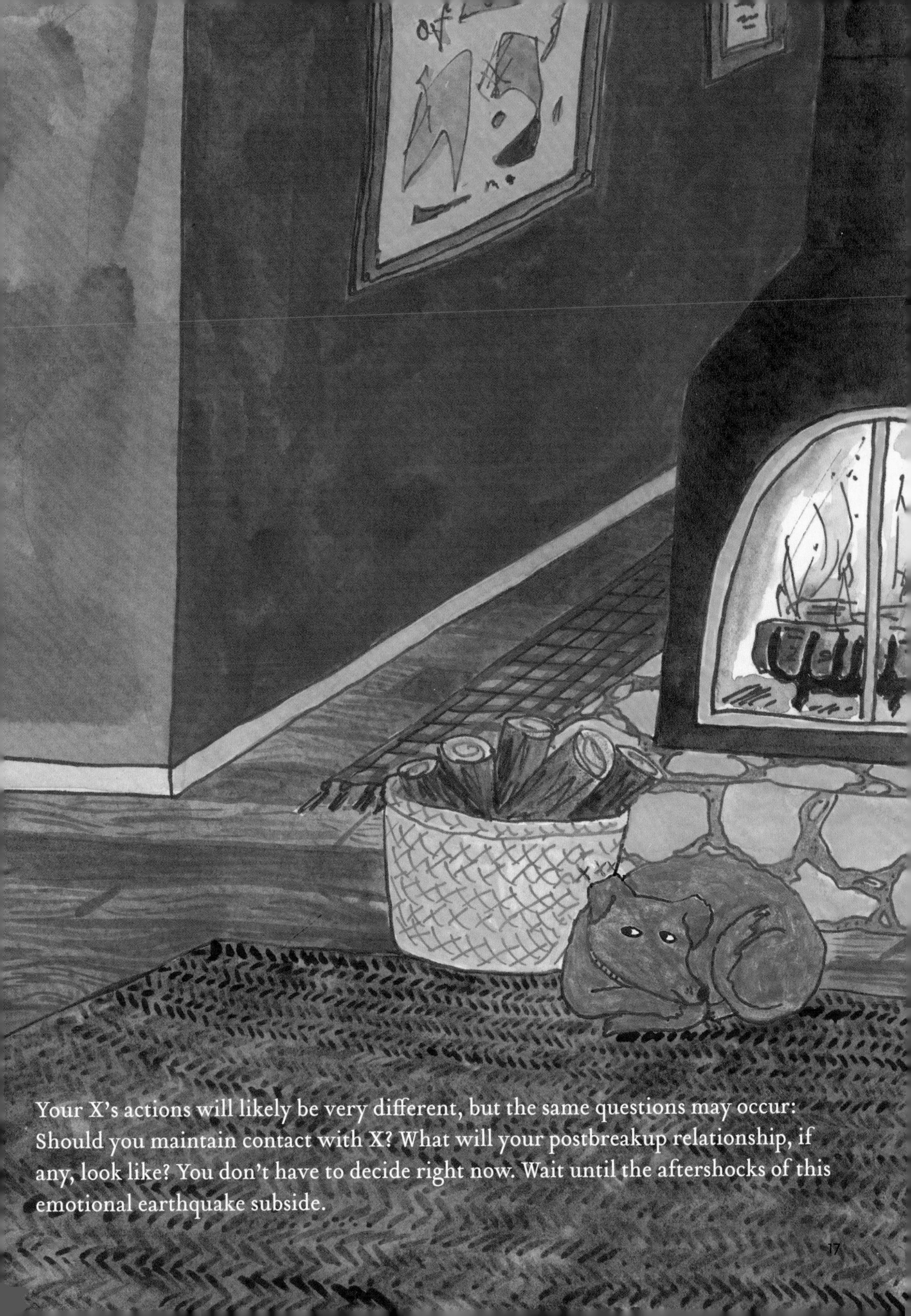

Your X's actions will likely be very different, but the same questions may occur: Should you maintain contact with X? What will your postbreakup relationship, if any, look like? You don't have to decide right now. Wait until the aftershocks of this emotional earthquake subside.

SO LET'S TALK ABOUT CRYING

You might cry for a day, a week, a month, or more.

Maybe you're a hideaway crier, able to keep the waterworks private. But if you're anything like me, tears will fall amid conversations with friends and strangers in grocery stores, on hiking trails, and during phone calls at work.

This will be disturbing to some, less so to others.

When you look back on this in the months and years to come, I hope that you won't be judgmental or embarrassed. Just think: Wow, I was in so much pain, I'm amazed I even survived.

HAPPIEST ABOUT YOUR CRYING

- X's new love interest
  - Your divorce lawyer
  (20 minutes of tears @ $400/hour = $133.33)
    - Your cat (breaks cat boredom)
      - Your moisture-loving plants
      (raises humidity in the room)
        - Tissue manufacturing execs

LEAST EQUIPPED TO HANDLE YOUR CRYING

- Man from the moving company who just wants to measure things
- Your realtor, trying to explain counteroffers while secretly counting down to cocktail hour far away from you
- Xs who abruptly dumped someone else last week or years ago
  - Passersby in the produce aisle

THINK THE WORST

List the worst things that have happened to you. I did this early on, compelled to see where X's exit ranked in the span of my lifetime:

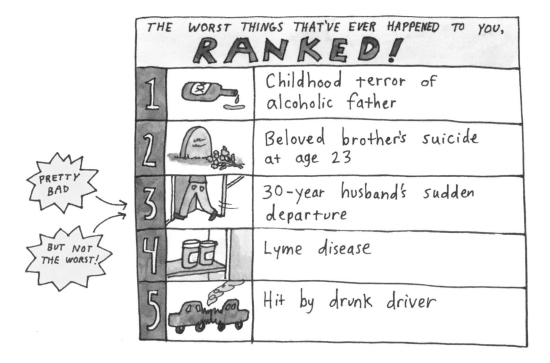

See, X's escapade isn't even at the top. It's only a middling mishap: Worse things have happened! If your Dumper's exit is at the top of your list, all I can say is, I'm so sorry. And also, you're probably much younger than I am. In time, X's exit will hold less emotional weight.

TAKE NOTES

Write in a journal, draw on cocktail napkins, or make voice memos, anything to record in some way what has happened. It will help confirm the reality of an otherwise surreal experience.

You may find that your memory is malfunctioning, so having a record that allows you to look back on this experience will help in several ways.

- It will prove that you weren't dreaming: This happened.
- It will remind you that yes, X really said those things.
- It will confirm the basis for your pain.
- It will help you see that you've made progress, however small.

This failed relationship is not your only story. It is one of many that make up your life, and in time, it will occupy less space in your mind and heart.

FIXATE ON THE HOW AND WHEN

People do awful things to one another, and sometimes the timing couldn't be worse. Ultimately, how and when it happened won't matter—but for a while, they can really hurt.

Hard ways to find out

Breathy phone messages or texts laden with anatomical wonders and sexy suggesti-cons

Credit card charge for an online dating app

Online photos where X and Y look much happier than you and X

X and Y actually doing it in your bed

BAD DAYS TO GET DUMPED

Your birthday

A major holiday you love

The day your dog dies

Two days before you retire

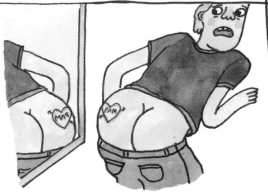

Any day after getting their name tattooed

Any other day of the year

FEEL YOUR PAIN

You may wonder,
"Have I hit rock bottom yet,
or will I just keep falling?"

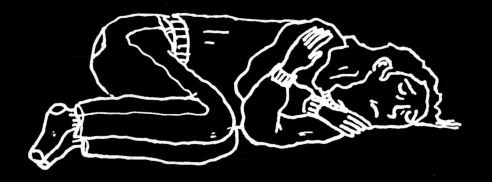

For help, call or text 988:
The 988 Suicide and Crisis Lifeline

Countdown: 1,570 days

STAY

You may think that there's no longer a reason to live. This is a tough one, because life-embracing reasoning springs from a healthy mind and body, and heartbreak can disrupt the whole system, leading people to think of bridge railings and train tracks and medicine cabinets.

As someone who has battled depression and lost a much-loved brother to suicide, I urge you to stay.

Not because your life is going to be perfect, but because—whether you believe it or not—your life touches others in ways you may never know.

Right now, you can't see the healing that is ahead. You can't imagine the love you might miss, and you can't know who you—after emerging from the depths of this pain—may be able to help in the future because of what you are experiencing now.

Empathy and compassion are nurtured here.

You're still not convinced? Try this: What if your best friend or child or anyone you care about was contemplating ending their life? What would you say and do to help? Do that for yourself. I beg you: Stay. There are better chapters ahead.

PART II

The Muddle

Against your will, you have joined a vast community of Dumpees. The good news: At a time when you feel most alone in the world, lots of other people will understand what you've gone through and how awful it feels.

Countdown: 1,569 days

JOIN THE CLUB

Statistically speaking and despite how you feel, you're far from alone.

Nearly half of U.S. marriages end in divorce. Marital infidelity, a wildly popular pastime, takes a toll. Married or not, unless you're both proponents of polyamory, adding a third person (or more) into the equation makes odds of dumping or getting dumped much higher.

Other factors bolster Dumpee ranks. Whether you're at peak energy in a new relationship or in a long-term relationship or married, the value you place on your partner and union may vary wildly from theirs. You may have started with shared goals but have grown apart or bored.

Plus there's a huge multiplier effect: Most people in the course of their lifetime have more than one romantic partner—from a handful to a roomful, if self-reporting can ever be believed. This makes getting dumped, and getting dumped more than once, a near statistical inevitability.

Welcome to our club, it's growing!

DISASTER	ODDS
STRUCK BY LIGHTNING	1 IN 500,000 (CDC)
HIT BY CAR	1 IN 4,292 (CDC)
DYING OF CANCER	1 IN 7 (NATIONAL SAFETY COUNCIL)
DYING FROM A FALL	1 IN 106 (NSC)
GETTING DUMPED AT SOME POINT	99.95 IN 100 (AUTHOR ESTIMATE)

SLEEP SIDEWAYS

One side of the bed is empty now. Someone else's warm body, maybe a body you adored, is gone, and it's a huge absence. If the bed is big enough, sleep sideways across the top half. This covers the gap, makes it easier to pull the covers on and off, and it's easier to make in the morning. If your feet stick out, wear socks.

MAKE A NEW TO-DO LIST

From the zombie-like zone of The Dumped, you are quickly forced to reenter the world of the living. Make a new list. If you have the energy to put only one thing on it, that's fine: Make a solid check mark next to that action ("Drink water"), and voilà, you've accomplished something. Tasks are tiny goals that help you focus on something other than your messed-up life.

Savor these accomplishments. If you are lucky enough to have food and shelter, and luckier still to have a dog or cat or sofa, you have everything you need to move forward—even if you don't believe that right now.

SPIN THE WHEEL

You may cycle wildly through a range of emotional states:

When will this nightmare end?

Scream, swear, harbor thoughts of revenge.

Dignity by a thread.

Change is the only constant.

Soon I will realize it's a mistake!

Tumble into a black hole.

DISBELIEF

RAGE

HUMILIATION

ZEN

MAGICAL THINKING

DEPRESSION

All of these conflicting emotions coexist in a messy mental heap. Eventually this emotional overcrowding will settle out and you'll better understand—to some extent, if not fully—why this happened.

TELL YOUR STORY

Who and how you tell people about the split is up to you. But do tell people who care about you. Keeping the split secret prevents you from receiving support from people whose level of understanding may surprise you.

Stick to the facts and keep it concise. Even if it were possible, you owe no one an explanation for something you can barely comprehend yourself. No one outside a relationship can know what has transpired between two people, even those within the relationship, in some cases. You may want to shape and share your story as a tale of criminal injustice, when you were simply with the wrong person. Or perhaps you were with an actual criminal, in which case I'm so sorry.

Some people—perhaps even family members—will react with words or actions in a way that makes you feel worse. It may help to distance yourself from them for a time, and yes, their feelings may be hurt.

Seek out relatives or friends who can help you safely adjust to or make sense of what just happened rather than adding to the chaos.

Those who can listen compassionately will be the most helpful. Over time, telling the story of what happened and how you feel may slowly help clear the storm of warring emotions enveloping you: rage, fear, disgust, shame, disbelief, grief, loneliness, hopelessness.

Given the high odds of getting dumped, maybe someday you can be an empathetic listener for someone else in need. But that day is far in the future. Now the focus is on regaining your footing.

Countdown: 1,524 days

ACKNOWLEDGE THE GHOST IN THE ROOM

The absence of X, particularly if you had an intense or lengthy relationship, can be so difficult.

- Their body may have felt like home to you.

- You may still hear their voice calling your name, though no one's there.

- They may appear in your dreams.

- You may turn to share something funny or earthshaking that the kids or dog did, forgetting that their chair or side of the bed is now empty.

All of this can be an ache for which there is no salve; only time will ease this particular pain. Being accomplished at something feels better than being an abject beginner—and you're new at being alone. It will get easier, but it takes practice. Think of it as paying dues on this new life you didn't ask for.

HONOR THE FLUX

Approaches to eating amid heartbreak:

- You eat anything and everything, swallow emotions you didn't know existed, and gain weight. Then you beat yourself up for yet another failure.

- You can't eat and lose weight. When people say you look terrific, you think, "I'm barely alive, this must be what it takes to look great!"

Over your lifetime, your body will change in so many ways; this is just another page in its ever-shifting story. Take long baths. Wear comfy clothes. Buy new pants. Appreciate all the parts and senses that still work.

Whichever way your appetite veers, go easy on yourself. Your body, with its fractured mind and heart, needs patience and gentle care right now.

Why bother to take care of a body no one wants? Whoa: You've veered into gross generalization. Yes, one person does not want it anymore, but you haven't heard from everyone else on Earth. There's a strong chance that someone will want it in the future, including you.

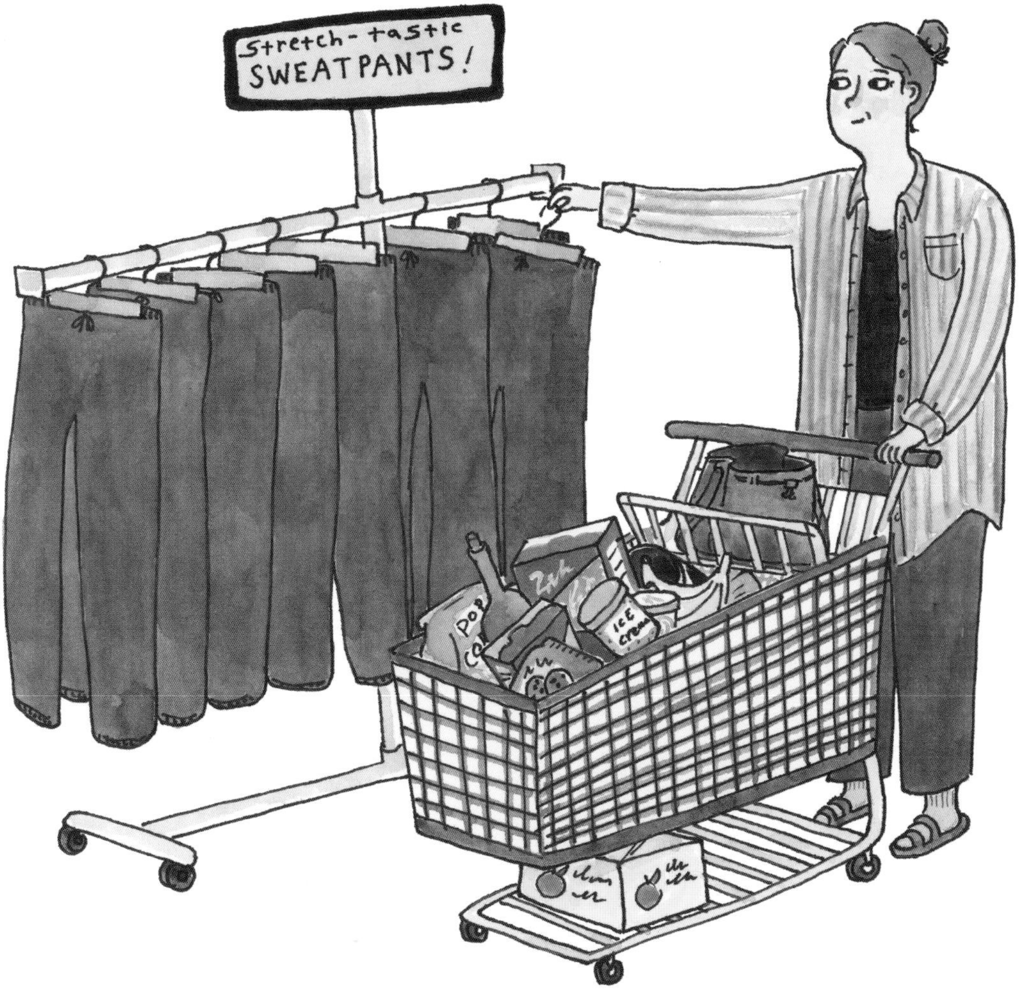
Stretch-tastic
SWEATPANTS!
POP
CO
ICE
CREAM

ASK FOR HELP

Such a major loss can rekindle emotions from older losses and hurts, painful feelings of guilt, shame, loneliness, and more. Past grief can even reemerge decades later when X dies, and along with X all the unresolved issues; thoughts about the partner or parent they were or could never be, for example, may boil up in anger and sorrow.

Sign up for therapy or grief support. Consider medication if depression persists.

FIGHT DENIAL

When you find yourself lonely and painting a rosy picture of yourself with X, don't lose sight of the facts.

Write yourself a note. Call it "What Was True." Only list what you know is true, not what you suspect or want to believe. Be specific. Did they lie, cheat, steal? Were they lousy in bed, a cat hater, a bad driver who screamed at other bad drivers?

Refer back to it when sad thoughts surround you.

WHAT WAS TRUE

1. Would rather be swarmed by bees than put the toilet seat down

2. Found it far easier to say no to you than to their mother

3. Even in the earliest years of your relationship, when you were the hottest you've ever been and ever will be, they suggested you lose a few pounds

4. Thought speed and efficiency were vital components in your sex life

5. Didn't notice when you left town for work, seemed surprised when you mentioned you'd been gone

6. Terribly forgetful (but only about deleting those secret voicemails and texts)

TAKE A SHOWER

Pretend you're a tree—a giant sequoia, not a weeping willow. Imagine that tree standing in the rain through centuries of storms, lightning strikes, fires. Stricken again and again, yet still standing.

Inside you may feel like you've been through your own century of storms, lightning strikes, and fires. It's hard to imagine now, but someday you'll be able to see yourself like that enduring tree with its resilient beauty. Meanwhile, stand tall in that tear-diluting rain for a long time.

While you're in there, grab a washcloth, lather on the soap, and scrub hard. You can't see it, but there's a new layer underneath waiting to emerge. How long will it take for your cells to replace the damaged ones, making you an all-new person? A while. Yet this relentless regeneration is happening day by day, even during the worst of this grief.

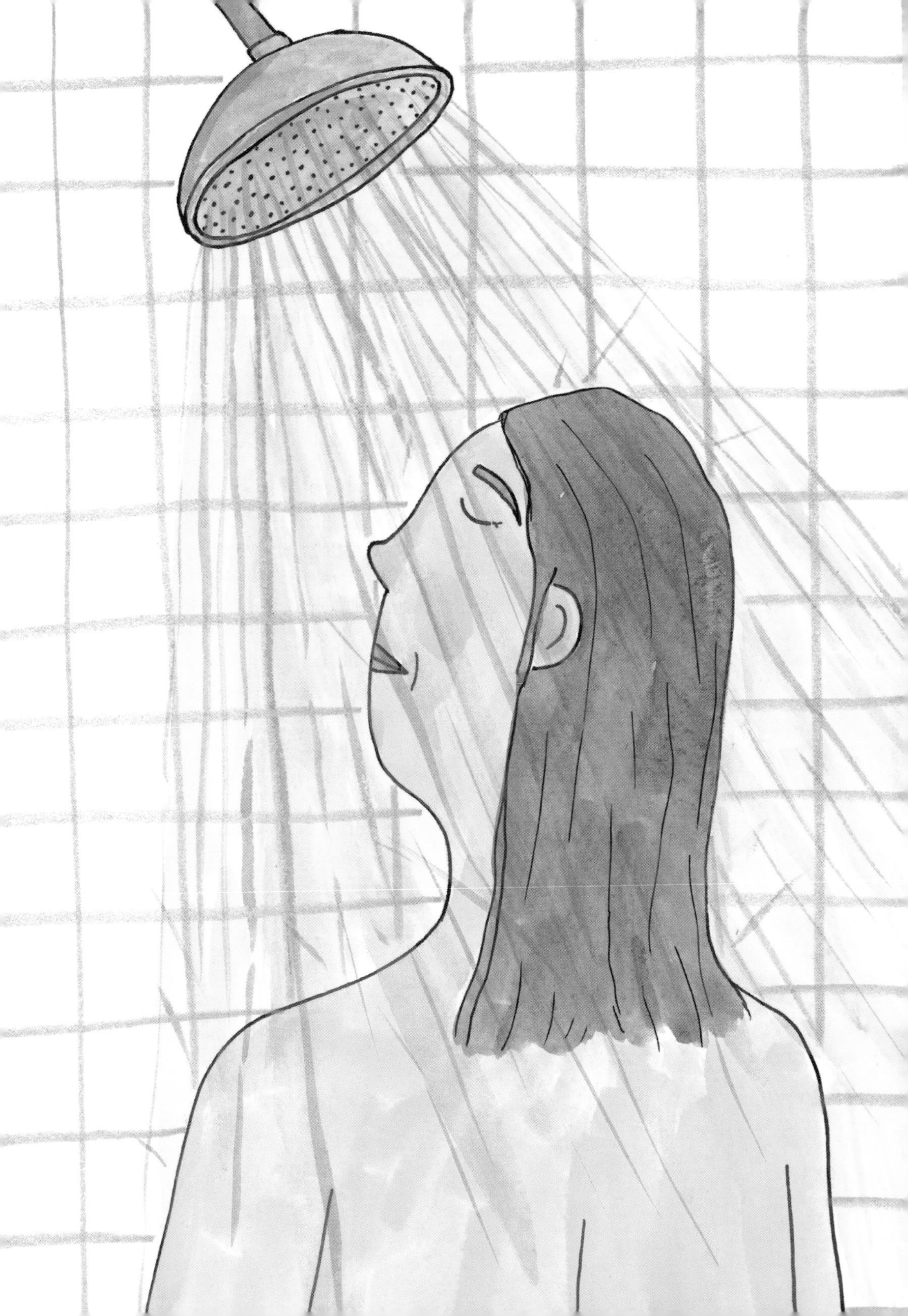

SET BOUNDARIES

imaginary
bubble of
protection
(color of
your choice)

Something big may happen—a mutual friend's death, a global pandemic, another needless war—and you realize that you can't talk about it with the one person you used to discuss almost everything with for months, years, or even decades. That can hurt.

Should you allow X in your life? If it's even a choice, this is a big decision.

In the short term, add distance if you need time to heal and figure out how to communicate effectively during this transition. Longer term, if children are involved, consider counseling to help establish a constructive new connection (or at the very least, nondestructive).

If children are not involved, and if any contact with X proves painful—reminders of your shared past, the sound of their voice, the omnipresence of Y—just say no.

It's nice to think that former partners can be friends, but when the pain exceeds the gain, it's not always possible.

HIRE CAREFULLY

You may need to hire a lawyer. It's another reality of separating marital or parental or business lives, converting your once-hot love affair to an ice-cold decree. Unlike in therapy, the why won't matter here. Only the how, how much, and who else is affected.

As in therapy, this will require you to reveal intimate events, information, and indignities to strangers when you feel least capable of doing so. Interview more than one lawyer, if possible, and choose carefully with help from people who have been through this already.

The good news? Your lawyer is your advocate when you need one most. And, if experienced, your lawyer has seen the worst of what people do to one another in the fallout of a failed marriage, and maybe—just maybe—your situation is better than that.

MAKE ANOTHER TO-DO LIST

You can aim a bit higher now.

Prepare a nice meal

wipe the Counter

take out the garbage

Check, check, check. Progress.

DISTRACT YOURSELF

Staying busy will help pass the time until the pain eases. Speaking from experience, some diversions are better than others.

HELPFUL

Exercising

Going to a job you like (or don't dislike)

Talking with friends about your loss — or anything but your loss

WILSONNN!

Watching movies where the star faces a fate far worse than being dumped and ultimately survives

UNHELPFUL

Jumping into a new relationship before taking time to think and heal

Publicly lambasting X in any forum (don't be a jerk even if X was a jerk)

Making hasty life decisions predicated on your current "nothing matters" mindset

Relying on drugs and alcohol to cope – losing yourself this way for more than a short time will affect your ability to recover and move on. Sadly, healing from heartbreak requires your full, unimpaired attention.

DISTINGUISH THOUGHTS FROM REALITY

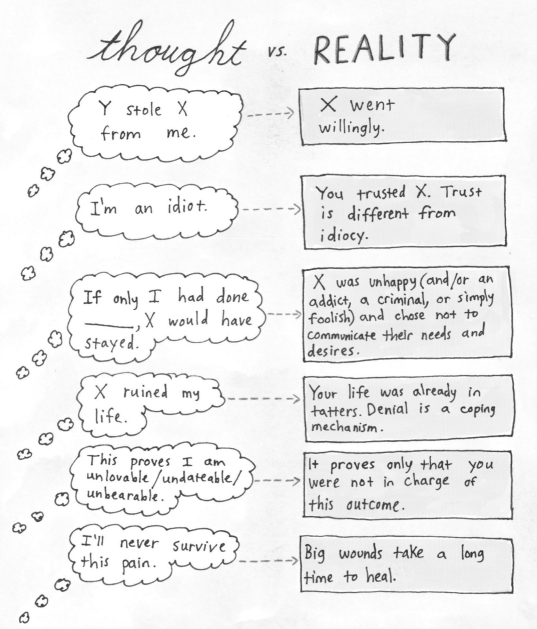

thought vs. REALITY

thought	REALITY
Y stole X from me.	X went willingly.
I'm an idiot.	You trusted X. Trust is different from idiocy.
If only I had done ____, X would have stayed.	X was unhappy (and/or an addict, a criminal, or simply foolish) and chose not to communicate their needs and desires.
X ruined my life.	Your life was already in tatters. Denial is a coping mechanism.
This proves I am unlovable/undateable/unbearable.	It proves only that you were not in charge of this outcome.
I'll never survive this pain.	Big wounds take a long time to heal.

Those thoughts bombarding you night and day may feel true, but chances are they're as far off course as your once-rosy love story.

HAMMER AWAY

Use a sledgehammer to break apart something you owned together. For me, it was a litter box, and surprisingly, it took quite some time. Far in the future your anger will fade dramatically, but now it needs a dramatic outlet. Wear safety glasses, and don't hold back. Recycle the shattered pieces of whatever you smash. Well done.

Countdown: 1,380 days

LISTEN

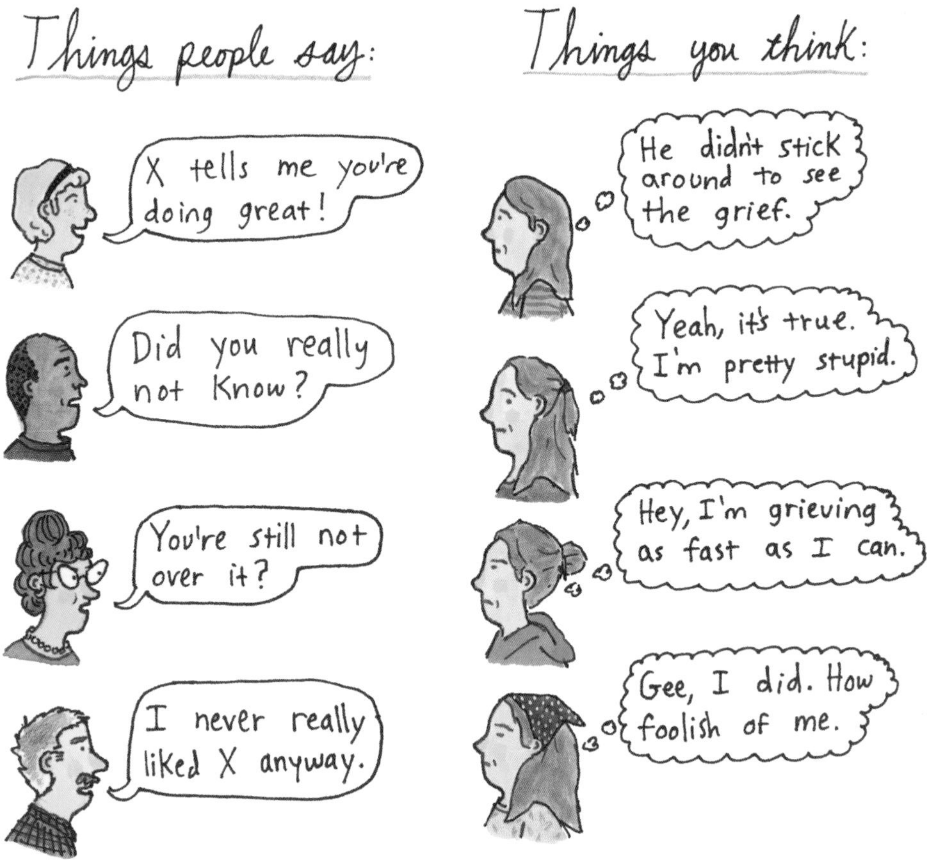

Things people say:
Things you think:
X tells me you're doing great!
He didn't stick around to see the grief.
Did you really not know?
Yeah, it's true. I'm pretty stupid.
You're still not over it?
Hey, I'm grieving as fast as I can.
I never really liked X anyway.
Gee, I did. How foolish of me.

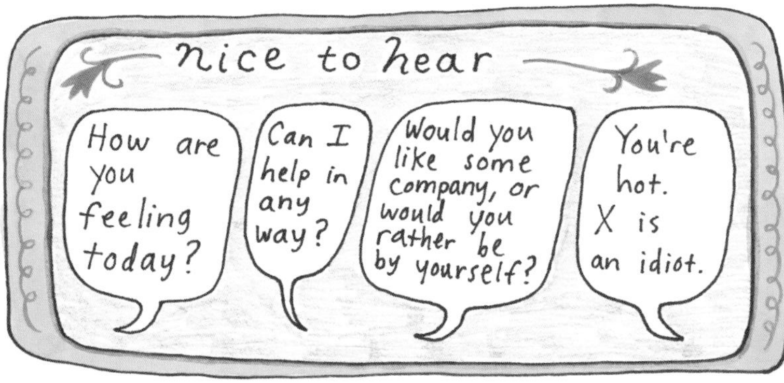

nice to hear
How are you feeling today?
Can I help in any way?
Would you like some company, or would you rather be by yourself?
You're hot. X is an idiot.

SCRUB IT

Get a rag and some cleaning solution and find a small surface in your home that's dirty, neglected, a bit downtrodden. Scour until it gleams. Pristine, unlike your messed-up life.

If you did this every day for a year, every surface in your home would sparkle, unlike your spirit right now. But maybe in the reflection you'd feel a bit brighter. More immediately, you'd have a clean place to put your toothbrush.

Countdown: 1,370 days

BRACE YOURSELF

The first anniversary of the day X dumped you.

When you are shown Y's photo and your sister says, "She Kind of looks like you."

The first time someone refers to X as "your ex," and it hadn't occurred to you because it still seems so soon.

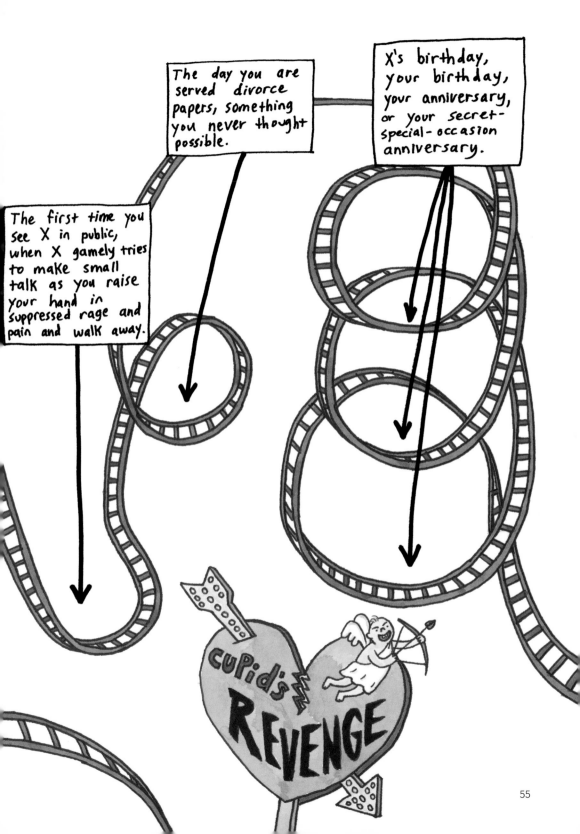

The day you are served divorce papers, something you never thought possible.

X's birthday, your birthday, your anniversary, or your secret-special-occasion anniversary.

The first time you see X in public, when X gamely tries to make small talk as you raise your hand in suppressed rage and pain and walk away.

CUPID'S REVENGE

FIND YOUR SONG

Did you and X have a favorite song? Maybe it played at your wedding, where those silly lifetime promises were made.

Cut a record-size circle out of a cardboard box. Write the song name on it in big letters. Then strike a match, hold "the record" over the sink, and watch it burn. Use care not to set the curtains on fire. Now find a new favorite song of your own. Take your time searching.

AVOID THESE SONGS

1. Patsy Cline, "She's Got You"
2. Dean Martin, "You're Nobody 'Til Somebody Loves You"
3. Eric Carmen, "All by Myself"
4. Three Dog Night, "One"
5. Toni Braxton, "Un-break My Heart"
6. The Righteous Brothers, "You've Lost That Lovin' Feelin'"
7. Bonnie Raitt, "I Can't Make You Love Me"
8. Al Green, "Tired of Being Alone"
9. Willie Nelson, "Sad Songs and Waltzes"
10. Tammy Wynette, "D-I-V-O-R-C-E"

LISTEN TO THESE INSTEAD

1. Carly Simon, "You're So Vain"
2. Kitty Wells, "Will Your Lawyer Talk to God?"
3. The Chicks, "Gaslighter"
4. Reba McEntire, "Take It Back"
5. Elton John, "I'm Still Standing"
6. Carly Rae Jepsen, "Party for One"
7. The Waitresses, "No Guilt"
8. Taylor Swift, "We Are Never Ever Getting Back Together"
9. Beyoncé, "Best Thing I Never Had"
10. Ariana Grande, "Thank U, Next"

BEHOLD THE BADGER

You are amazing. A strange creature by virtue of being human, but an amazing one, with your funny nose, oddly shaped ears, body that grows and shrinks and shifts with the seasons and years.

You would not look at a badger and say, "What an ugly badger—just look at its bulging stomach and odd eyes." You would appreciate its uniqueness: the adorable stripes, the squatty yet confident stance. You would not pass judgment on a badger. Why are we so prone to do it to people? Let's take care of ourselves, and the badgers, too, with some basic respect.

Don't make the mistake of thinking that because X dumped you, you are less than you should be, that you don't measure up. X may have left for reasons that had nothing to do with who you really are, how you look, the uniqueness of your character. Though it feels as if you were in the crosshairs, it's possible you were not even in X's field of vision.

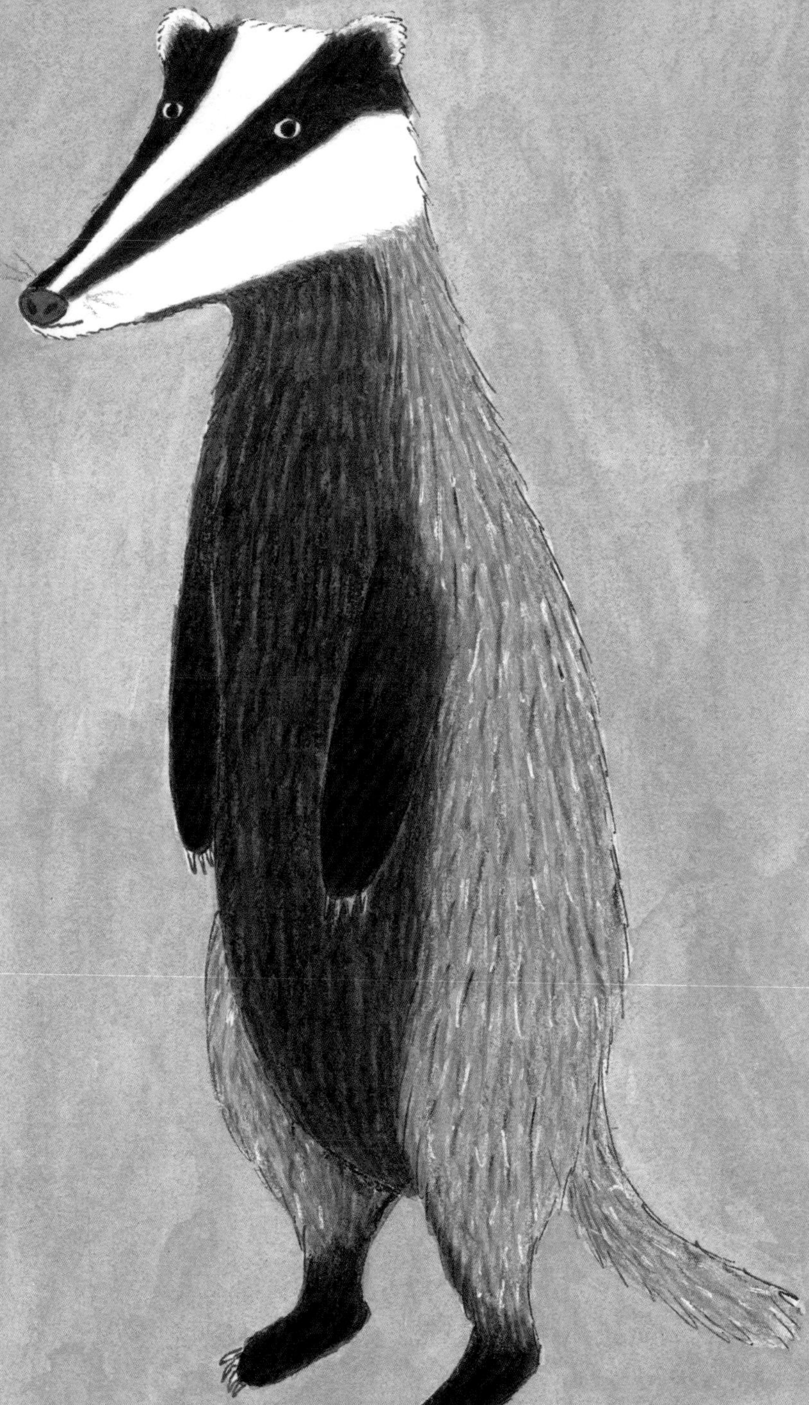

TAKE COMFORT

You didn't have a choice in being born. It was someone else's doing. Now you do have a choice—not about being dumped but about deciding to move forward. The dumping is history. Chances are, by the time you heard about it, it was old news, at least to X.

There is one similarity to the day you were born: You were crying then, and you may be crying now. But the dry season isn't far away. The bad thing happened, and it's done. It is in the past, was in the past from the moment it happened, and it can't happen again in the same way.

Stand in the sun and let it embrace you.

FINISH IT

Practice finishing anything. Finish a sentence, a sandwich, a letter to a friend, the laundry.

Look at you. A period of time has passed in which you didn't die of grief, loneliness, anger, or fear. If you can survive this, imagine what else you can do.

DITCH THE GROOVE

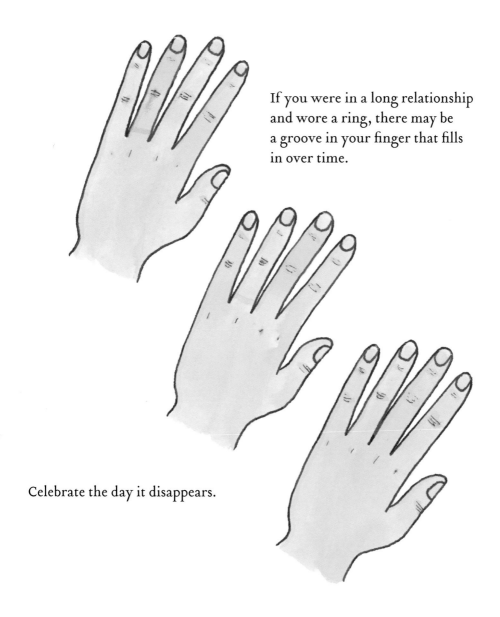

If you were in a long relationship and wore a ring, there may be a groove in your finger that fills in over time.

Celebrate the day it disappears.

Countdown: 1,240 days

WEAVE A NET

The absence of X may feel like a lost safety net: emotional, financial, social, or otherwise. But maybe that net came at a higher cost than you knew. Maybe you gave up important parts of yourself, or even lost the person you felt was the authentic you—the one you liked. You are walking solo now, an unskilled trapeze artist of sorts, which can be scary.

If you have children and a job, life may carry more responsibility and pressure, particularly if finances are strained. If you're single with fewer obligations, finding a middle ground between alone and lonely may be challenging. If you're older and part of the surging "gray divorce" trend, alone may be new and bewildering. But all these paths eventually can lead to new experiences in which you find solace and satisfaction.

Trust your ability to begin to weave your own safety net, one that will be far stronger than you can imagine, with the help of those who care about you. You can handle this, even if it feels impossible right now.

Countdown: 1,212 days

LIGHTEN UP

Maybe you will leave a home you've loved, or move to another community or state. This may entail an emotional walk through memorabilia of a lifetime together. Sell, give away, or leave behind anything that, by connection to that memory-strewn lost world, prevents you from moving forward.

HIDEOUS LAMP
Gift from his mother, always hated it

PICTURE FRAMES
Held photos of the life we used to share

WEDDING DRESS
Purchased by mistake, apparently

CUTESY PAINTING
Wedding gift from friends who also divorced post-infidelity

OVERSTUFFED CHAIR
Ass that used it is gone

MAKE ONE MORE TO-DO LIST

Your capacity for moving forward is growing.

Check, check, check. Progress.

Countdown: 1,188 days

GIVE IT TIME

Imagine yourself walking barefoot at the warm edge of the ocean, glancing behind now and then to watch the tide erase all traces of your passage.

All is temporary: the moments of joy and sorrow, the presence or absence of a loved one. All will change, which means that as sad as you still feel, it won't always be this way.

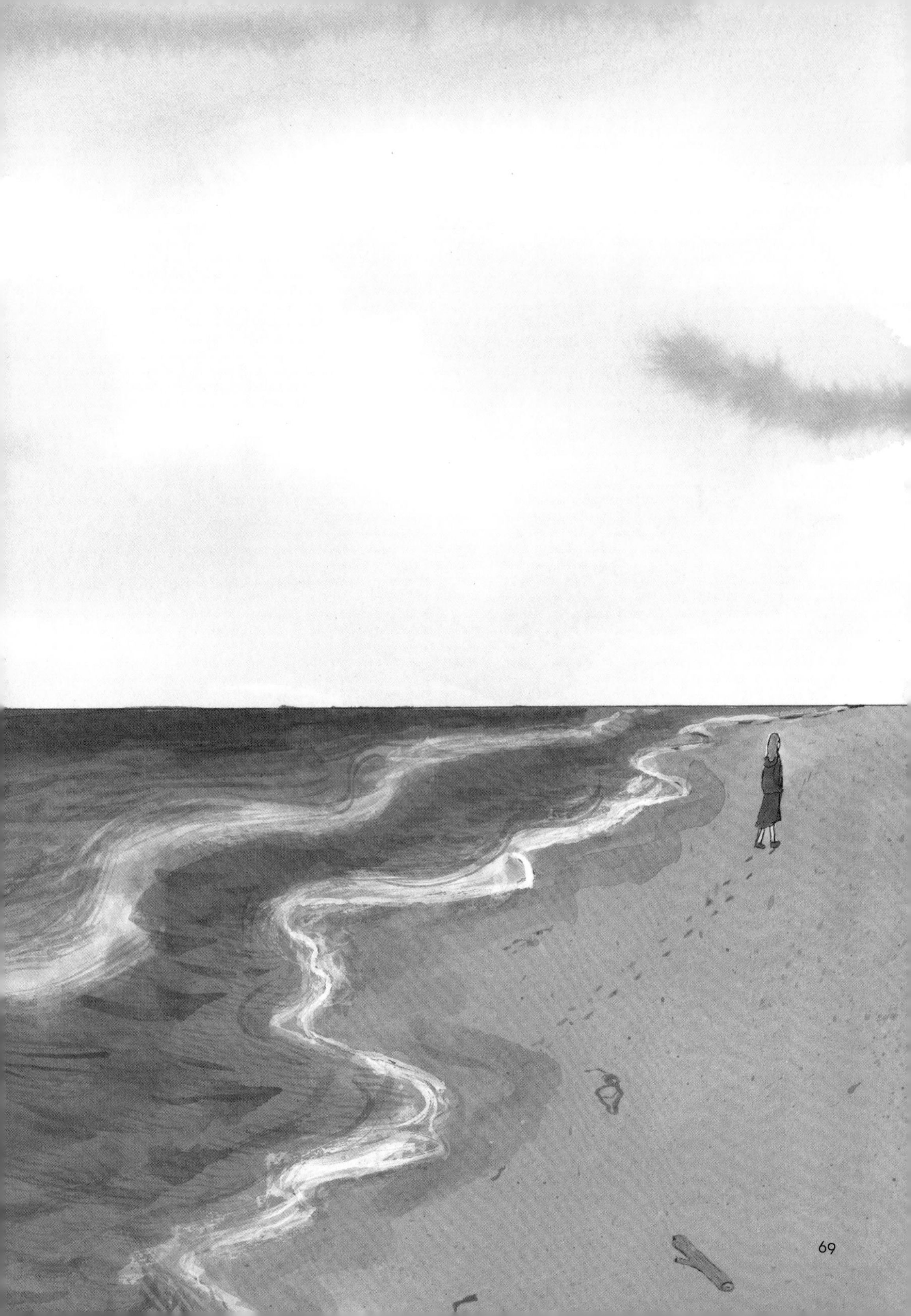

PAVE IT OVER

Each trip to a place you experienced with X may draw old memories and feelings to the surface. Try revisiting a few of those places on your own or with friends: a favorite restaurant or music venue, a beloved vacation spot, a small town or big city where you've always enjoyed playing tourist. Over time, creating new memories will help you stop tripping over the old ones.

SAY THANKS

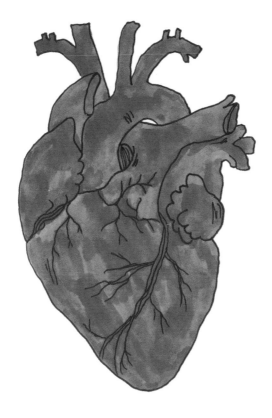

As more months pass, look in the mirror at your body, wrinkled or smooth, fat or thin, freckled or speckled, young or old. Say, "Thank you for carrying me through that awful time."

Give special credit to your battered heart, which continued to beat one hundred thousand times a day throughout, a miracle of efficiency, adaptation, and endurance. You're making progress, with more to come.

NOURISH YOURSELF

The best thing about cooking is that you control
the outcome. It doesn't have to be great, just edible.
You can cut vegetables violently, and no one
will be the wiser. Just watch your fingers.

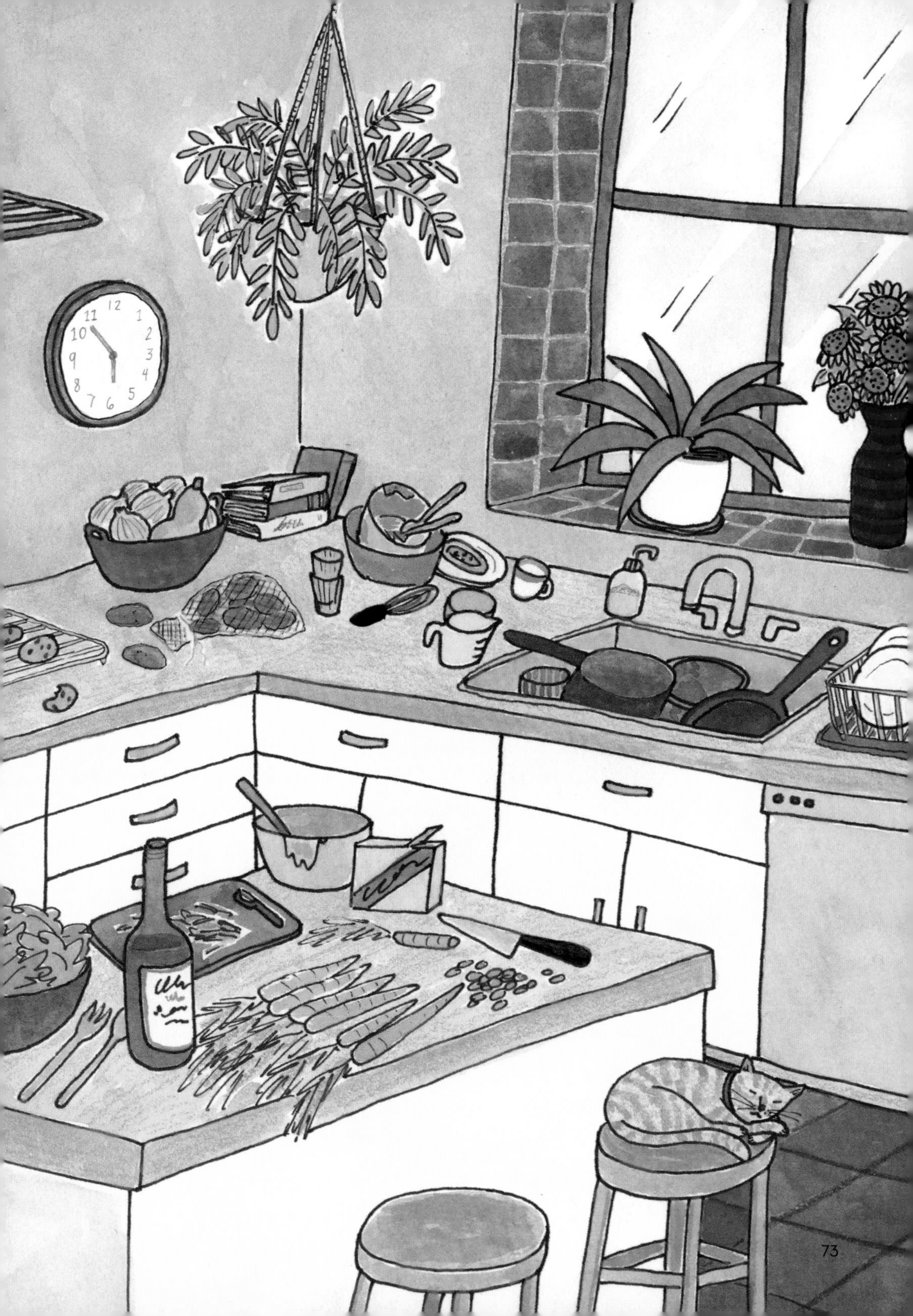

Countdown: 1,136 days

MAKE YET ANOTHER TO-DO LIST

Remember when the only thing on your to-do list was to pull the covers over your head? You've made great progress, even if it has taken a long time to get to this point.

Now, plan something fun, maybe even a bit daring or unexpected. Is there something you really want to do but are hesitant? Shift your thoughts from "I hope to" or "I think I might" to "I will." There, you have a plan!

SPEAK YOUR TRUTH

Maybe it's time to embrace real-speak—honesty in all communication, paired with kindness—particularly if X's deceit is part of your tangled pain. After key interactions, ask yourself, "Did I say what I meant? Is it what I honestly believe?"

Communicating openly and honestly may increase your ability to protect yourself, to say no when needed, and to forge healthier relationships in the future.

INVITE TRANSFORMATION

Getting dumped is a blow to one's self-esteem and even your identity. Did you surrender key aspects of yourself during this relationship?

What you remember about the predumped you—how you typically thought, felt, or behaved—is not necessarily who you are in this moment or who you will be a year from now. You are capable of far more change than you know.

SHIFT YOUR ATTENTION

If you remain focused on X, after a while it becomes a habit, a choice of sorts. Every ounce of energy expended in that direction hampers your progress. Imagine X in the rearview mirror of your car as you drive away, becoming ever smaller and eventually out of sight.

Even if you are still connected to X in a redefined relationship, that history with all its sad or bitter memories will recede as your new life expands. At the end of each day, instead of dwelling on old thoughts, think of two things you noticed that were interesting or beautiful. It could be something that happened (friendly comment at the grocery store) or a pretty sight (honeybee dipping into a flower).

Noticing will help you move toward appreciation, then gratitude. Which is a big improvement over heartache, but it takes practice. Sorrow will come regardless; joy you need to create.

BLAME IF YOU MUST . . .

When you fall in love with someone, you sign on to a package deal without being able to see the whole package. X showcases their smile, wit, and sense of fun. It can be hard to see their biases, the consequences of how they were raised, genes for addiction, and so much more. Who can blame you for picking the wrong person when you haven't had access to such essential information?

My reality:
You lied and cheated.
You didn't talk to me.
You were never home.
You never wanted to make love.
You didn't care about me.

If you cling to the notion that they really were the right person, your one-and-only true love, you are wrong: Their absence is the proof.

X's reality:
You were always angry.
You constantly criticized me.
You didn't want to spend time with me.
You never wanted to have sex.
You didn't care about me.

. . . BUT KNOW THAT IT'S NOT ALWAYS SIMPLE

My childhood reality:
I saw so much violence.
I was scared.
I never told anyone.
I lived with shame.
I was lonely.
What I needed didn't matter.
I needed unconditional love.

X's childhood reality:
I heard that I was always wrong.
I lived with shame.
Crying was seen as weakness.
Anger and conflict were hidden.
I was lonely.
What I needed didn't matter.
I needed unconditional love.

Countdown: 980 days

AIM FOR BALANCE

Adjusting to life without a partner to share in work and decisions may be easy for you—or far more challenging than you expected. It's a bit like learning to juggle: Keeping all those flying objects in the air while maintaining your balance is hard.

Keep practicing. You can do this, even if you lose your grip sometimes.

HAVE FAITH

You may find faith in a higher power, in nature's unending cycles of renewal, or in your continued ability to adapt and grow in the months and years ahead. Seek it out, invent it, whatever you need to do. Then lean into it as a vital support.

Like the future, you can't know what shape it takes, but you can acknowledge the promise it holds; within that lies hope.

We're here for a relatively short time, but long enough to realize how much is unknowable, how much is beyond our control, and how much mystery interlaces human relationships.

Unknowable: How long we'll live, what another person is really thinking, your favorite sports team's chances, the depth of your reservoir of trust for future relationships, what will happen tomorrow.

Beyond our control: Unexpected disasters on the highway, in the sky, midocean, or mid–living room; another person's reaction to our offerings of love or affection; time.

Mystery: What really attracts people to one another? Why is it so difficult to make our needs known and understood? Where do ducks sleep at night?

DON'T FORCE A BOW ON IT

With time, you may be able to see more clearly your part in the relationship. Where you gave too much or didn't give enough. Where you expected too little or too much, tolerated bad treatment or doled it out, were sexually cold or hot or somewhere in between.

Lower your expectations that some of these issues—your role, your feelings about X and why they did what they did—will ever be resolved in an emotionally satisfactory way. Some things may never be.

Sometimes the best you can hope for is that X and X's behavior ultimately become irrelevant to your new life.

CONSIDER YOUR OPTIONS

With this restart button (the one you did not push) you've been given a choice. What kind of person do you want to be: angry, bitter, and focused on the past? Or open to learning, taking this blow as instructional? Embracing "bitter and angry" as your new strategy—vowing not to let anyone else get close enough to hurt you again—will not be helpful in relationships with others or with yourself.

This experience can teach you who to avoid. And that when someone shows they don't care for you, believe them the first time and move on; actions mean so much more than words.

If you decide to take a zero-trust approach, review that stance over time. Meanwhile, at least consider the opposite strategy: being vulnerable, trusting, and open to being hurt again, as hard as that can be. If you wall yourself off, you may miss the reward of real intimacy with a person who cares.

Trusting again is like rowing a battered boat around the bend of an unknown river. It's a bit scary. You must constantly adapt, holding the oars steady amid ever-changing currents, on your way to safer shoals.

PART III

The Beginning

You are graduating into your new life. Time to dump the "Dumpee" designation and see your situation in a new light: You have been released, set free to create a life of your own choosing.

REWRITE THE SCRIPT

You have recovered enough to see that the future is waiting. What will you do? What lifestyle do you really want? And what can you do to move in that direction? If you had only a year to live, how would you want to use that time?

Minute by minute, day by day, you are writing your own future with your thoughts and actions. Someone else may have been partly in control of the narrative before—or so you may have believed—but now you hold the red pen. That's the one

editors use to scribble changes that may be unwelcome but necessary.

You are now in charge of writing your own script. What kind of movie would you want a starring role in? Rom-com? Adventure film? Sports epic? Porno flick? Sci-fi complete with hot alien?

OWN YOUR DESIRE

To no longer have sexual expression with a once-loved partner is a huge loss. Your needs and desires for love, comfort, and sexual intimacy don't die with the relationship. Acknowledging and meeting those needs is important but, amid grief, may feel impossible. And who can you talk to about this? Even when talking to a therapist, it can be an uncomfortable subject.

Think about what you really want and need as another part of caring for yourself. How to do it? Hook up online? Order sex toys in brown-paper packages? How can you fulfill your need for intimacy and physical connection?

It's okay if this is challenging new territory: Like so many others, you will find your way through.

MAKE IT PERSONAL

Make a list of your interesting qualities, and another list describing the person you hope to find.

ME

- Hazel eyes, thick hair, outsized second toe
- Sarcastic, rarely cry these days, enjoy picking up trash
- Enchanted by hummingbirds, frogs, and geese
- Revel in language, judgmental about poor spelling
- Movie night with popcorn plus *dog* equals bliss

YOU

- Kind eyes, hair optional, any size toes
- Good sense of humor, nice to restaurant servers
- Enjoy meandering hikes, slow museum strolls, long kisses
- Love animals of all kinds, badgers included
- Movie night with popcorn plus dog equals bliss

SHOP AT THE USED-PARTNER STORE

Maybe you slept around a lot after the breakup. Or maybe you haven't been on a date in thirty-five years. At some point you may decide to try online dating—what I think of as "shopping at the used-man store." You may orient differently or want to shop elsewhere. Wherever you choose, be brave, and pack your patience.

Even if you don't meet the person of your dreams, having people like your profile can be encouraging (ego boost, fifty dollars for three months). Meeting people and realizing that you have no interest in them also can be oddly empowering. Now you get to press the reject button.

BEWARE OF SCAMMERS

Scammers are everywhere, with lines like: "My friend is looking over my shoulder and likes you, my subscription is about to run out, he's a good-looking guy . . . etc." Profiles with only one photo, poor syntax, and misspellings are also clues.

Be careful online and in person. Before your online chats move to phone or video calls, ask for their full name and confirm their identity. Are they a real person in sync with what they've told you? Can you find other online photos matching listed photos?

This process is a tremendous time-saver because it rules out almost everyone.

NO WARRANTY
NO GUARANTEE

GO ON A BAD DATE

When you're ready to date again, prioritize your comfort and safety, then lower your expectations. Odds are this will be a bad date, or at the very least, mediocre. Your date may never stop talking, never start talking, or have trouble finding their mouth with the soup spoon. They may raise their red flags boldly, or show no red flags but their spirit just seems a bit . . . rumpled.

A bad date is good because it sets this new bar low. You realize you don't have to waste time pretending to be someone you're not or like what you hate. It's fine to be just who you are as you search for common ground and interests, fun and mutual attraction—even if there's none available.

Once this lousy date is over, celebrate. You did it. You tried. Be proud of yourself for taking a chance, extending yourself toward the unknown and all its untapped potential. Just remember: This is only the start. A hurdle that you cleared, a test of your mettle. The next time will be easier. And if you continue to be this brave, there might even be a great date in your future.

Who will you choose?

AVID ANGLER

- Man of mystery! His face is hidden in all photos by hat, sunglasses, and dangling fish.
- Dating him is an ocean breeze! He'll be out with his fishing buddies 98 percent of the time.
- Knows all the right lures, except when it comes to women.

FITNESS FAN

- This spandex-clad beefcake is guaranteed to raise your heart rate!
- What a romantic: He knows his soulmate is out there and she's definitely a size 2.
- Impressive working knowledge of steroid pharmacology.

NEGATIVE GUY

- Doesn't want to text more than twice before moving on to a phone call and, ideally, your bed.
- Doesn't want ANY DRAMA (defines drama as almost any communication with a woman).
- By strange coincidence, every single one of his exes is "crazy."

WEAPON LOVER

- He's hunting for love, along with numerous endangered species.
- Has never met you but vows to "protect you" with lethal force.
- Aiming for a traditional woman who knows "her place."

THE EXHIBITIONIST

- Eager to show you his naked body from a host of artless angles.
- This free spirit shucks all housekeeping along with his clothing — giving him more time to introduce you to his creepy hobbies.
- Nothing will ever come between you, especially fabric.

MAN IN CONTROL

- World's easiest date! Check your autonomy at the door, babe — this hunk makes all the decisions. You'll be having steak.
- He's planned your first three dates and has already picked out your wardrobe and "safe word" too.
- Explains in his profile that he's used to getting what he wants even though he's clearly having trouble getting a date.

97

Countdown: 555 days

GATHER PROOF

Did you strike out online and conclude you're undateable? Perhaps you forgot that there are billions of people in the world. If you've lost sight of your lovability, ask an honest friend to share the good and interesting things they know about you. Unless you are a serial killer or other horrific human variant, there's someone out there who will be enchanted by your weird and wonderful ways.

Whatever the outcome, in whatever venue, give yourself credit for trying—for being brave enough to go forth, in all your imperfect humanness, in search of friendship, partnership, and love.

Take a photo of yourself with a friend, even a four-legged one: proof of love. You are loved, therefore you are lovable.

RELISH YOUR SINGLEHOOD

Watching couples in public or while socializing may help you appreciate being single. At the very least, you can be grateful that you're NOT . . .

. . . wearing a trite matching shirt

. . . eating together in dead silence

. . . shopping with a reluctant companion

. . . arguing over chairs in IKEA

. . . married and terribly jealous
that your friend is single

LOOK BACK

Open your journal or get out those cocktail napkins or voice memos with notes from just after you'd been dumped. You'll be amazed at the gap between then and now.

Maybe you have not found a new partner (do you really want a new partner?), but you will have grown in so many ways. Just know that even years later, this review may be a bit painful—triggering old feelings from that time. How long will it take for the pain to go away? More.

Meanwhile, begin to treat yourself as someone who loves and admires you and can't wait to spend time with you.

SCREAM

Anger and sadness from this loss may interrupt at odd intervals, long into the future, shattering your newfound composure. As part of grieving, it defies any schedule. Breathe deep, scream, and then move on.

FAKE IT

Maybe you never had much self-confidence. Or maybe you did, but this loss left it in the shadows. Shedding cultural and familial patterns, judgment, and biases, including your own, isn't easy, and rejection can feel like a pile-on. Whoever told you that you weren't good enough was wrong. You are, even if you don't believe it right now.

The good news: You don't have to wait for someone else to make you feel better. "Fake it till you make it" can work wonders. That may mean pasting on a smile while lying in bed alone as you face another wearying day of reinvention.

Be kind to someone who needs it. Give a stranger a compliment out of the blue. Take your neighbor some warm cookies. Reach out to a friend you've lost touch with. At some point you will be on the receiving end, but for now, the trick is just to get on the path by acting like a loving, caring human being.

TRY IT ON

Go to the thrift store and pick out a set of clothes that you like and that make you feel like a different person. Drive to another town where you don't know anyone. There, you can pretend to be a different person—who do you want to be? If it involves a cool hat, all the better.

Countdown: 434 days

SEEK BEAUTY

Where do you find beauty? In books, nature, art, music, conversation, friendship?
Pursue more of it.

If you need inspiration, visit a museum showcasing works of great Renaissance artists. Many of those artists faced the sad double whammy of nursing a broken heart in an era of terrible sanitation. Yet somehow they managed to leave so much beauty behind.

Countdown: 414 days

DRAW YOUR DREAMS

Get a whiteboard or unfurl a big roll of paper. Write on the board or paper the words "BIG DREAMS" up top in big letters, and underneath, define them in detail. Your dream lifestyle, dream partner, dream job, dream future.

Be as specific as possible. Before you write it down, ask yourself, is this the biggest I could dream? Are you saying "take a watercolor class" instead of "create a watercolor masterpiece"? Filter out all the ifs, ands, and buts. Write whatever you feel, no matter how much it scares you. You don't have to show anyone; this is for your eyes only. Dream big, then take a photo.

WRITE A LETTER

Write yourself a nice note, put a stamp on it, and mail it. Face it: It's exciting to get a handwritten letter from anyone these days.

FIND FELLOWSHIP

You're in a safer emotional place now, and other people have something to teach you. Years later, they may be happy to share—knowing it could help you, as it did me—how they made it through their own heartbreak.

You will hear sadness and commonality and accounts of the long road to healing, along with tears (sometimes years later) and a bit of embarrassed laughter. And again, you learn that you are not alone.

LET GO

What has been sucking away your time and attention, even while providing what feels like much-needed distraction? Social media, your phone, TV. Will those things help or hinder your plans for yourself?

Review and whittle it all down to those few things that really serve you. Letting go is self-care, and while you may be new at this, it can make it easier for you to pursue new goals. Imagine the world as an old-time radio rife with static—so much noise. Turn it off and tune in to you.

Countdown: 275 days

CULTIVATE LIFE

I love gardening for much the same reason I love being a parent: It allows me to play a part in an unceasing miracle, the cycle of life.

You plant a garden with near-microscopic seeds, and, barring a plague of pests or targeted tornado, you can reasonably look ahead to a day when the plants will yield a harvest. Tending it requires patience and steady care, and results aren't guaranteed, though you can educate yourself and gain new skills to improve the odds.

Healing from heartbreak is a bit like that. Happiness isn't a matter of instant gratification. You're working toward it, piecing together happy moments and days as you build a new life.

Gardening tip: Plants that get cut back severely—which one assumes would be against their will, if they could only express that—often come back stronger the next year.

FORGIVE OR FORGET

Do you need to forgive X to move ahead?

Everything I read indicated yes, noting that forgiving X doesn't mean you agree with their actions—simply that you acknowledge what happened and "let go of anger." Much of it was peppered with the implication that a really good person would, of course, readily forgive.

This felt like yet another demand on top of the rest: leave my longtime home, rebuild my trap-door life, reimagine my future, grieve alone.

What mattered most, I decided, was strengthening my own ability to move forward—working to release my attachment to someone with whom a reciprocal relationship was not possible. Perhaps forgiveness, like grief, keeps its own schedule.

 In the interim, forgetting has its own allure.

ONE SPRITZ
AND IT'S LIKE IT
NEVER HAPPENED

Countdown: 143 days

GIVE YOURSELF A GIFT

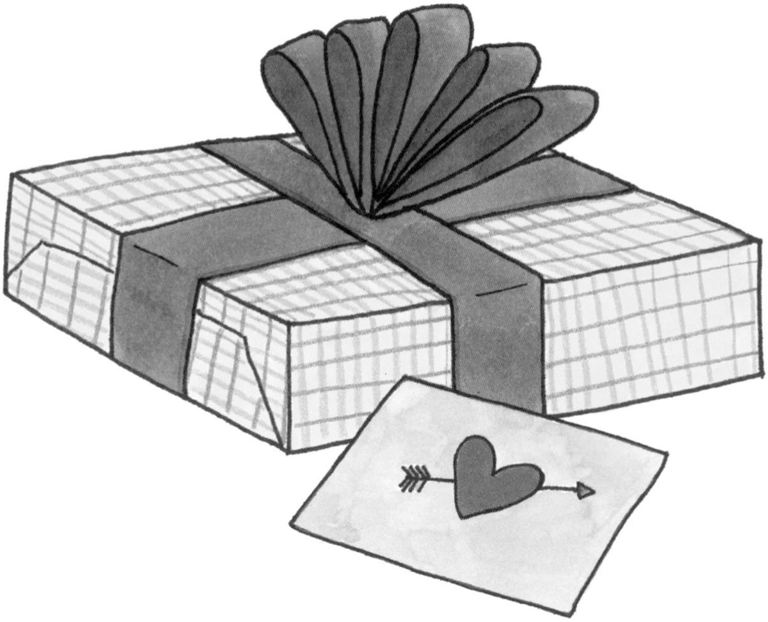

Order a little gift and have it gift-wrapped. Attach a loving note. Open it with suitable fanfare.

Acceptance is a long process that includes taking ownership of your situation, your life. Treat yourself kindly along the way.

DON'T WAIT

To wear the new clothes. To smile at the grocery clerk who's dealt with too many nasty people today. To run naked through the sprinklers because it's hot (hey, neighbor!). To say what you mean, without being mean.

SAY YES

Practice stepping outside your comfort zone without worrying about what might go wrong. Worrying about the worst doesn't stop it from happening. Try the reverse: Consider the best possible outcome. It's more fun and statistically, at least, equally possible. Plus, you never know where saying yes will lead.

EXPECT THE UNEXPECTED

- You may train to become a hospice volunteer, which by a strange twist leads you to fall in love with a Labrador retriever puppy (outcome: daily walks, devoted movie-and-popcorn companion).
- You may spend a big birthday on a remote Minnesota lake (outcome: kayak skills).
- You may raise chickens (outcome: quiche).
- You may get a tarot reading as a gift from your daughter (outcome: you write a book).

PART IV

Unbroken

The day you unbreak your heart may be a day much like any other. It can sneak up on you, this realization that your life has been freshly painted with new colors, depth, and meaning.

Countdown: 0 days

For me, the turning point came during an early morning walk.

Against an early spring sky, I looked up to see six Canada geese flapping close overhead in a 5-1 formation, honking wildly. In the lone bird I saw myself, flying alongside memories of our former family of five.

Moments later, three more geese flew even closer in a perfect V, beauty and purpose in motion. My three children, I was reminded, were the beautiful result of those years.

I chose that moment, more than four years in the making, to unbreak my heart.

You have choices too.

This life is yours alone, rare and singular, the responsibility of no one else. What you do with it next will be bolstered by the knowledge and understanding you have gained, along with new compassion for yourself.

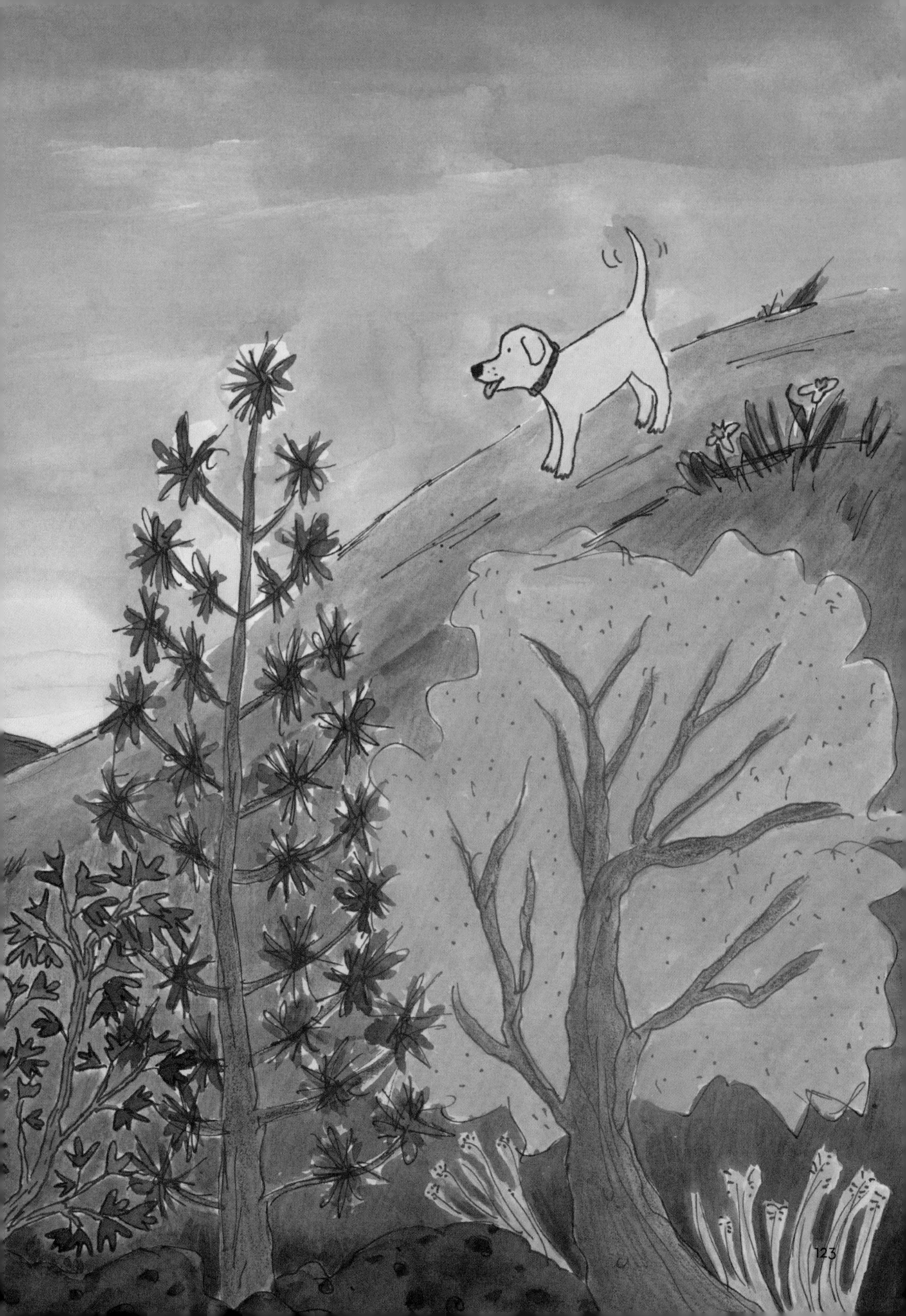

Understand that you are beautiful in all your complexities and imperfections, your quirks and eccentricities and experiences.

That those complexities and experiences led you here, to this new place of hard-won growth and wholeness.

That your heart is not only unbroken but stronger for what it has endured.

And that you are worthy of lasting love.

Acknowledgments

Thank you to our wonderful agent, Kate McKean at Howard Morhaim Literary Agency, for your steadfast advocacy and caring partnership. And to Nancy Miller and her incredible staff at Bloomsbury—Harriet LeFavour, Laura Phillips, Myunghee Kwon, and Patti Ratchford—for your savvy editing and trust in us. Creating such personal work is a vulnerable thing; having a supportive team means the world. We're so happy our book found such a loving home at Bloomsbury.

FROM SUZY

To Martha and Kathie in California, Kris in British Columbia, Wanda in Missouri, and Ian in France: Thank you for sharing how you healed after being dumped. Your candor and encouragement convinced me that this book was needed.

Gratitude also to early readers Maria Barrs, Joan Jackson, Lisa Mayers, Gail Ringen, and Kathie Smith. Your comments, suggestions, and friendship helped me push forward.

Heartfelt appreciation to my siblings and their spouses—Ann and Lee, Mark and Joy, and Michael and Luann—for being there when I most needed you. Thanks especially to Ben, Hallie, and Nick for your steadfast love and support amid the challenges of navigating your parents' divorce. My heart is with you always.

And to Hallie, as we wrap our second collaboration: Thank you for your kindness, patience, and insight that led this book to final form, and for your creativity and skill as an artist whose work can still move me to tears—the good kind.

FROM HALLIE

Thank you to my mom. You had a lot of options for what to do with your broken heart. You could have stuffed down your pain or weaponized it against the world. But you are the classy, brilliant Suzy Hopkins. So of course you took your pain, felt it deeply, healed it slowly, and wove your story into something poignant and funny and deeply generous. I'm in awe of you and your beautiful, unbroken heart. And thank you for watching Max and Nora, your brand-new grandchildren, while I write these acknowledgments in the next room.

Thank you to my husband, Jack, for your love and reassurance throughout the long and emotional journey of making this book. I am so grateful to be married to someone so kind, funny, hot, and willing to offer color consultations, anatomy drawing lessons, and Photoshop help.

To my babies: This book was drawn over the span of my pregnancy, and I'll always remember it as such a joyful and happy experience. Also, I appreciate you arriving after I completed all the artwork. Your timing is impeccable.

I'm so grateful for my family and friends—you know who you are—who helped me get through my parents' divorce, and then also helped me get through making the book about the divorce. Talking, crying, and laughing with the people I love is a vital part of my creative process, and I'm incredibly lucky to have each and every one of you in my life.

A Note on the Author and the Illustrator

 Suzy Hopkins is a former newspaper reporter and magazine publisher. She is coauthor of *What to Do When I'm Gone* (2018, Bloomsbury) with her daughter, illustrator/writer Hallie Bateman. She lives in Cincinnati, Ohio.

 Hallie Bateman is an illustrator/writer whose work has appeared in the *New Yorker*, the *New York Times Magazine*, The Awl, and many others. Her books include *Directions* (2021, Workman Publishing), *What to Do When I'm Gone* (2018, Bloomsbury), and *Brave New Work* (2015, Museum of Modern Art). Other books she has illustrated include *Eggasaurus* (2022, Simon & Schuster). She lives in Cincinnati, Ohio.